LIVING A FAITH THAT MATTERS

A 30-DAY DEVOTIONAL ABOUT FOLLOWING JESUS AND IMPACTING OUR WORLD

40-DAY BIBLE STUDY SERIES

PETER DEHAAN

Living a Faith that Matters: A 30-Day Devotional about Following Jesus and Impacting our World

Copyright © 2019-2023 by Peter DeHaan.

All rights reserved: No part of this book may be reproduced, disseminated, or transmitted in any form, by any means, or for any purpose without the express written consent of the author or his legal representatives. The only exceptions are brief excerpts, and the cover image, for reviews or academic research. For permissions: peterdehaan.com/contact.

Unless otherwise noted, Scriptures taken from the Holy Bible, New International Version®, NIV®. Copyright © 1973, 1978, 1984, 2011 by Biblica, Inc.™ Used by permission of Zondervan. All rights reserved worldwide. www.zondervan.com The "NIV" and "New International Version" are trademarks registered in the United States Patent and Trademark Office by Biblica, Inc.™

Published by Rock Rooster Books, Grand Rapids, Michigan

ISBN:

- 979-8-88809-049-7 (e-book)
- 979-8-88809-068-8 (paperback)

Credits:

- Copy editor: Robyn Mulder
- Proofreader: Julie Harbison
- Cover design: Cassidy Wierks
- Author photo: Chelsie Jensen Photography

Selected readings from books 1 to 10 in the 40-Day Bible Study Series:

- *Dear Theophilus*: copyright © 2019 by Peter DeHaan
- *Dear Theophilus*: copyright © 2019 by Peter DeHaan
- *Dear Theophilus, Isaiah*: copyright © 2020 by Peter DeHaan
- *Dear Theophilus, Minor Prophets*: copyright © 2020 by Peter DeHaan
- *Dear Theophilus, Job*: copyright © 2020 by Peter DeHaan
- *Living Water*: copyright © 2021 by Peter DeHaan
- *Love Is Patient*: copyright © 2021 by Peter DeHaan
- *A New Heaven and a New Earth*: copyright © 2022 by Peter DeHaan
- *Love One Another*: copyright © 2023 by Peter DeHaan
- *Run with Perseverance*: copyright © 2023 by Peter DeHaan

To all who want to live a faith that matters

Books in the 40-Day Bible Study Series:

- Dear Theophilus (the Gospel of **Luke**, formerly That You May Know)
- Dear Theophilus, **Acts** (formerly Tongues of Fire)
- Dear Theophilus, **Isaiah** (formerly For Unto Us)
- Dear Theophilus, **Minor Prophets** (formerly Return to Me)
- Dear Theophilus, **Job** (formerly I Hope in Him)
- Living Water (**John**)
- Love Is Patient (**1 and 2 Corinthians**)
- A New Heaven and a New Earth (**Revelation**)
- Love One Another (**1, 2, and 3 John**)
- Run with Perseverance (**Hebrews**)

CONTENTS

Jesus and Living a Faith That Matters	1
Day 1: Jesus: The Word, the Life, and the Light	3
Day 2: A Child Is Born	7
Day 3: Celebrate Jesus	11
Day 4: Jesus and Justice	15
Day 5: Judgment or Mercy?	19
Day 6: Be Like Jesus	23
Day 7: Be like Jesus, Part 2	27
Day 8: Help Others	31
Day 9: Love Your Neighbor	35
Day 10: Love One Another	39
Day 11: Count the Cost of Following Jesus	43
Day 12: Prophecy Fulfilled	47
Day 13: Job Responds to Bildad	51
Day 14: Jonah's Confession	55
Day 15: Bildad Provides Something to Consider	59
Day 16: Jesus Is the Way	63
Day 17: We Are on the Winning Side	67
Day 18: The Final Sacrifice	71
Day 19: Wait for It	75
Day 20: A New Covenant	79
Day 21: Confess Our Sins	83
Day 22: God's New Creation	87
Day 23: Dealing with Theological Disagreements	91
Day 24: No Divisions	95

Day 25: Run with Perseverance	99
Day 26: Devoted to Jesus	103
Day 27: Holy Spirit Power	107
Day 28: The Revelation of Jesus	111
Day 29: The Alpha and Omega	115
Day 30: Coming Soon	119
The 40-Day Bible Study Series	123
For Small Groups, Sunday School, and Classes	125
If You're New to the Bible	127
About Peter DeHaan	131
Books by Peter DeHaan	133

JESUS AND LIVING A FAITH THAT MATTERS

Jesus is the star of the Bible. The Old Testament points to him and the New Testament reveals him.

Jesus is also the theme for this collection of devotionals. They're selected from the first ten books of the 40-Day Bible Study Series, with three readings from each book.

Like the Bible, this 30-day devotional will point you to Jesus and tell you about him, all through the lens of Scripture. In doing so you can grow closer to him and be inspired to live a faith that matters.

May the Holy Spirit speak to you as you read each day's meditation. As you do, may you love Jesus more fully and impact the world around you for his Father's glory.

DAY 1: JESUS: THE WORD, THE LIFE, AND THE LIGHT
JOHN 1:1–14

In him was life, and that life was the light of all mankind.
(John 1:4)

The book of John opens with a most moving passage. It's lyrical, it's evocative, and it is exquisite.

In this poetic prelude of John's Gospel, he calls Jesus the Word, and asserts that the Word *is* God. This means Jesus is God. While some people may think it's an overreach to claim that the Word refers to Jesus, keep reading.

To remove all doubt, John later states that this Word becomes human to join us on earth. Jesus becomes a man to live among us. Jesus, as the Word, shows us his glory as the one and only Son from Father God. Jesus overflows with grace and abounds in truth. He is the Word sent to us from God.

We often assume the Word of God means Scripture. But remember that the New Testament of the Bible didn't exist until several centuries after Jesus's death and resurrection. Because of this, we should consider God's Word as his *spoken* Word, more so than his *written* Word. What if Jesus is more than the metaphorical Word? What if he serves as the actual Word of God? Yes, Jesus is the Word.

John also writes that in Jesus is life. Jesus is present when time begins and takes part in forming our existence. In fact, without Jesus, creation cannot occur. Physical life flows through Jesus at creation. In the same way, eternal life emanates through Jesus now. Jesus comes so we may have life and live with abundance (John 10:10). This theme of life recurs throughout the book of John, with his writing mentioning life in forty-one verses, more often than any other book in the Bible.

The life *of* Jesus, and the life *through* Jesus, gives us light. Just as the sun that Jesus created illuminates

Living a Faith that Matters

our physical world, the light that Jesus gives off now illuminates our spiritual world. This light shines for us in the darkness that surrounds us, exposing the evil in our world. Best of all, this light of Jesus overcomes the darkness, pushing it away. This means good is stronger than evil. God is more powerful than Satan. Hold on to this truth. Don't forget it.

Jesus is the light. As the light—our true light—he comes into our world to save us. Though many do not recognize him or accept him, everyone who receives him and believes in his name become children of God, born of God.

Because of Jesus we've been born into the physical realm, and through our belief in him we are born a second time into the spiritual realm.

Take time to contemplate John's profound opening to his biography, revealing Jesus as the Word, the life, and the light.

Do you recognize Jesus as Word, life, and light? Do you believe in him?

[Discover what else John says about the Word of

God in 1 John 2:14, Revelation 1:1–2, Revelation 19:12–13, and Revelation 20:4.]

Today's reading comes from *Living Water: 40 Reflections on Jesus's Life and Love from the Gospel of John*.

DAY 2: A CHILD IS BORN
ISAIAH 9

For to us a child is born, to us a son is given, and the government will be on his shoulders. And he will be called Wonderful Counselor, Mighty God, Everlasting Father, Prince of Peace. (Isaiah 9:6)

The book of Isaiah contains many prophecies that look forward to Jesus, the people's promised and much-anticipated coming King. In what may be the best known of these prophecies, Isaiah gives us amazing and comforting characteristics about our future Savior, Jesus.

Isaiah starts by saying that Jesus will come as a child, God's gift to us. Father God will send Jesus to us as an infant, who will grow up to become our supreme ruler for the rest of time.

Though Isaiah doesn't specifically call him *Jesus*, the prophet does give us four other awesome names.

First, we'll call him *Wonderful Counselor*. Though anyone can give advice, not all advice is good, and some is even bad. Not so with Jesus. His words will come forth as instructions of a most amazing nature, possessing a distinguished authority.

Mighty God emerges as a second title for Jesus. Yes, Jesus is God. Beyond being godlike, Jesus will possess all of God's characteristics, including being almighty.

Jesus's third title builds upon his second one: *Everlasting Father*. This is a bit confusing because if Jesus is God's Son, how can he also be the Father? But remember that Jesus and the Father are one. What we see in one, we see in the other. However, let's focus on the word *everlasting*. Jesus is eternal, transcending all time. He participated in creation, and we will celebrate him in the new heaven and new earth, which is to come.

The fourth name for Jesus is *Prince of Peace*. He will usher in an era of perpetual harmony, ruling with excellence for the rest of time.

Last, this child—Jesus, whom God will send—will grow up to rule us. As a descendant of King David, Jesus's government will have no end, for it will extend into eternity. And, unlike human rulers with their frailties, Jesus will oversee his people with perfect, flawless justice.

Jesus is more than our Savior. He is our eternal King, who will usher in peace and rule with perfect justice for all time without end.

Do we stand in astonished awe of who Jesus is and what he has accomplished and will accomplish?

[Discover more about Jesus's characteristics in Luke 4:32, John 1:1–3, John 14:9, John 17:21, Revelation 21:23, and Revelation 22:16.]

Today's reading comes from *Dear Theophilus, Isaiah: 40 Prophetic Insights about Jesus, Justice, and Gentiles.*

DAY 3: CELEBRATE JESUS
LUKE 2:1–20

"I bring you good news that will cause great joy for all the people." (Luke 2:10)

Joseph and his pregnant fiancée travel to Bethlehem for a mandatory census. Unable to find a place to stay, they hunker down in a barn. There, among the filth of livestock, Jesus is born. This is the first Christmas.

Each Christmas my attention focuses on Jesus, the real reason for our annual celebration. In considering the first Christmas, my thoughts are warm and cozy, happy and joyous, idyllic and serene. Angels sing, kings give gifts, and awed shepherds do their shepherding thing.

But all this misses that Jesus is born in someone else's barn, amid unsanitary conditions, and with the stench of animal feces filling the air. It seems so unholy, so unworthy. There's no medical team to monitor Mary's condition or aid in the birth. It's likely just Mary and Joseph trying to figure out what to do. Mary likely helped with the birth of other babies, but I wonder how much Joseph knows about the delivery process. Yet despite all this, Jesus is born.

Once the trauma of delivery passes and the messiness of birth is cleaned up, I envision an awestruck Mary gazing lovingly at this miracle that God produced in her. While nursing him, she strokes his cheek and whispers, "I love you," as only a mother can do.

As Mary overflows with joy and basks in amazement over what God has done, out in the fields a bunch of shepherds are doing their job, unaware of what has happened. Suddenly an angel shows up. He begins by saying what most angels say when they appear before humans, "Don't freak out." Even so, understandably so, the shepherds tremble at his glory. Then the angel says, "Newsflash: A baby has just been born in Bethlehem. He's the Savior. The Messiah you've been longing for." He

Living a Faith that Matters

tells them what to look for: a baby swaddled, abed in a manger.

Then, to underscore the validity of the angel's message, a grand angel choir appears. They chant their praise to God, giving him all glory and blessing the earth with the peace of his favor.

The shepherds rush to Bethlehem to check things out. Just as the angel said, they find the proud parents watching over the baby boy, Jesus, who's sleeping in the animals' feed trough. After confirming what the angel had told them, the shepherds leave and tell everyone they meet about the angel's message and Jesus's birth. Then the shepherds head back to their flocks in awe of God and what he has begun.

The shepherds believe what the angel told them, seek confirmation, and then tell everyone, praising God in the process. They're the world's first missionaries for Jesus. After they leave, Mary grows introspective, pondering and cherishing all these events in her heart.

What do we do with the good news of Jesus? Do we tell others or keep it to ourselves?

[Discover more about Jesus's birth in Matthew 2:1–23.]

Today's reading comes from *Dear Theophilus: A 40-Day Devotional Exploring the Life of Jesus through the Gospel of Luke*.

DAY 4: JESUS AND JUSTICE
ISAIAH 41–42

"Here is my servant, whom I uphold, my chosen one in whom I delight; I will put my Spirit on him, and he will bring justice to the nations." (Isaiah 42:1)

After giving us four chapters of historical narrative, Isaiah shifts back to more prophecy. His future-focused look tells us about Jesus.

Though Jesus is God's Son, as our Savior—the Messiah—he is also God's servant, who will come to earth in service of Father God to restore us into a right relationship with him. God chose Jesus to redeem his people, for God delights in him.

Under the power of God's Spirit, the Messiah

will champion justice. This justice isn't only for the nation of Judah, but it's for all nations—all people, everyone. This Savior will not proclaim his message with loud, boisterous words but with gentleness. He will protect the weak and encourage those who struggle.

Jesus will faithfully promote justice, never wavering from his mission. Through his followers, both then and now, he will persist until he spreads justice throughout the entire world.

Centuries after Isaiah's prophecy, when Jesus comes to earth, he will come to heal and to save. Today most people seek Jesus for his saving power, while two thousand years ago people came to him more for his healing power.

Where does justice fit into all this?

The people in the Old Testament expected that the promised Savior would come as a military leader to rescue them from their oppressors. They assumed he would be an actual king, in the line of King David, ushering in an era of justice. They believed that at his arrival, the Jews would finally receive fair treatment meted out by a morally righteous leader. He would be true in all he does, governing his people with excellence and protecting them from the immoral oppression of ungodly leaders from opposing nations.

Most of us don't see Jesus today as a physical Savior but as a spiritual Savior. However, throughout the world, many people struggle under the weight of oppressive regimes. They need physical deliverance. They seek the Savior who will provide them with justice. They need Jesus.

We all do.

Do we view Jesus as our savior, healer, or provider of justice? Can he be all three?

[Discover more about justice in Psalm 89:14, Proverbs 16:10, Jeremiah 21:11–12, Matthew 12:17–21, Matthew 23:23, Luke 18:3–8, Hebrews 1:8–9, and Revelation 19:11.]

Today's reading comes from *Dear Theophilus, Isaiah: 40 Prophetic Insights about Jesus, Justice, and Gentiles.*

DAY 5: JUDGMENT OR MERCY?
HOSEA 3–4

"I will not punish your daughters when they turn to prostitution, nor your daughters-in-law when they commit adultery, because the men themselves consort with harlots."
(Hosea 4:14)

Hosea rants against spiritual prostitution and adultery. His words seem to morph into a double meaning, implying both a spiritual and a physical application.

God says that he won't punish the people's daughters when they turn to prostitution. Nor will he discipline their daughters-in-law when they commit adultery. The reason? They don't engage in these acts alone. The men participate, too, taking a lead role.

In a spiritual sense, this implies that the person who leads someone else into spiritual adultery deserves greater punishment. But the person who follows them into it will go unpunished.

Now let's look at the physical aspect. We start with the Law of Moses. He writes that when a man commits adultery with another man's wife, both the man and the woman must die. A common form of execution in that day is stoning.

Fast-forward to Jesus in the New Testament. The Pharisees have this rule from Moses in mind when they bring a woman caught in the act of adultery to Jesus. They ask what he thinks about Moses's command that she must die by stoning. Though their query seems legitimate, they're trying to trap Jesus. They want to maneuver him into saying something they can use against him.

Jesus sees through their ruse. He doesn't answer their question directly. Instead, he gives permission to anyone who is without sin to pick up the first rock and hurl it at the adulterous woman. Since no one is sinless, one by one they all slink away in humiliation. In this way, Jesus offers the woman mercy as opposed to judgment.

This also serves as a reminder not to judge others for their sins because we have sinned too.

However, there's another element to this story. Where's the guy? It takes two to commit adultery, right? Why did the Pharisees only haul in the woman and not drag the man before Jesus? It's because they have a double standard. It may even be that one of their own was the adulterous man. In their minds, the woman deserves death, but the man's involvement isn't worth noting.

In economic terms, there needs to be both supply and demand for a market to exist. This applies to prostitution and adultery. Society and the church tend to focus on the *supply* side of the fornication equation. God's focus seems to be on the *demand* side.

From both the spiritual and physical perspective, the person who initiates should receive punishment. At the same time, the other person, though not guiltless, receives mercy.

How does this unexpected passage in Hosea inform how we should respond to sexual sin, specifically prostitution and adultery?

[Discover more about what the Bible says about prostitution and adultery in Leviticus 20:10, Proverbs 6:26–29, and John 8:3–11.]

Today's reading comes from *Dear Theophilus, Minor Prophets: 40 Prophetic Teachings about Unfaithfulness, Punishment, and Hope.*

DAY 6: BE LIKE JESUS
ISAIAH 61–62

The Spirit of the Sovereign Lord is on me, because the Lord has anointed me to proclaim good news to the poor. He has sent me to bind up the brokenhearted, to proclaim freedom for the captives and release from darkness for the prisoners, to proclaim the year of the Lord's favor and the day of vengeance of our God, to comfort all who mourn, and provide for those who grieve in Zion. (Isaiah 61:1–3)

Isaiah prophetically tells the people that the coming Savior—who we now know is Jesus—will move in Holy Spirit power. He will:

- proclaim good news to the poor,
- bind up the brokenhearted,

- declare freedom for the captives and release from darkness for the prisoners,
- announce the year of the Lord's favor and the day of vengeance of our God,
- comfort all who mourn,
- provide for those who grieve, and
- bestow on them a crown of beauty instead of ashes.

Wow, this is quite an impressive list. There's at least one thing there that will resonate with everyone.

Now let's jump forward several centuries to the New Testament. We can read what Jesus has to say about these prophetic words in Isaiah. Here's how the story unfolds.

On the Sabbath, Jesus goes to the synagogue in his hometown to worship God with family and friends. It's his turn to read Scripture, and the day's reading is from Isaiah.

Jesus stands. The synagogue leader hands him the scroll that contains the words of Isaiah. Jesus unrolls it, almost to the end. He reads the passage that we now know as Isaiah 61:1–2. The people are familiar with these words. They've heard them before, and

Living a Faith that Matters

they're anxious for this prophecy to happen. They hope it will occur in their lifetime. They sure do need a Savior to rescue them, to set the oppressed people free—because they are certainly oppressed.

After Jesus reads the passage, he rolls up the scroll, hands it back to the synagogue leader, and sits down. Everyone looks at him, waiting to hear what he has to say. His message isn't long or elegant. It's succinct but powerful. "Today this prophecy is fulfilled." I'm sure there are some shocked gasps when Jesus says this.

These prophetic words from Isaiah are what Jesus will do. It's a mini job description: under the power of God's Spirit, Jesus will speak truth to those who are seeking, provide help to those in need, and give hope to those who hurt.

As Jesus's followers, we should be like him. We should do what he did. It will take a lifetime to put these things into practice. Therefore, God leaves us on earth after we decide to follow Jesus. Being like Jesus and telling others about him is what we should do with our remaining time here.

If we love Jesus, we need to do what he would do. And just as with Jesus, it begins with the Holy Spirit, and we can start today.

How can we put these things into practice? How can we implement one of these actions to help others?

[Discover more about Jesus's job description in Luke 4:16–21.]

Today's reading comes from *Dear Theophilus, Isaiah: 40 Prophetic Insights about Jesus, Justice, and Gentiles.*

DAY 7: BE LIKE JESUS, PART 2
1 JOHN 2:3–6

Whoever claims to live in him must live as Jesus did.
(1 John 2:6)

Today's passage talks about knowing God and keeping his commands. If we claim to know God and don't do what he says, we're only deluding ourselves from the truth, and our claim is false. But when we obey his commands our love for God is complete.

In short, as his followers, we must live as he lived. We must be like Jesus.

We are fortunate to have four biographies of Jesus in the Bible to inform us about how he lived. They are the books of Matthew, Mark, Luke, and

John. By reading them we know what Jesus does during his time here on earth. Then we can follow his example and be more like him.

We don't have to follow a bunch of rules with legalistic fervor or adhere to an extensive list of ritualistic commands like we find in the Old Testament. We must simply be like Jesus. It's that easy.

Here are some of the things that Jesus does:

- Jesus makes his relationship with his Father a priority. From an early age, Jesus puts his Father in heaven first (Luke 2:49). This is what matters most.
- Jesus takes care of himself so that he can take care of his followers. Jesus knows that if he isn't spiritually healthy, he can't expect to be at his best to help others (Matthew 14:23).
- Jesus has time for everyone who comes to him. While going to heal Jairus's daughter, he pauses to heal a sick woman (Luke 8:40–56). He stays in Samaria for two extra days simply because the people ask him to (John 4:40).

- Jesus teaches others about God. Jesus speaks with authority and not like other religious leaders (Mark 1:22). He instructs people using parables (Mark 4:2). His longest message in the Bible is the Sermon on the Mount (Matthew 5–7).
- Jesus heals others (Matthew 8:14–15). And he says his followers will do the same (John 14:12).
- Jesus opposes religious hypocrisy (Luke 13:15).
- Jesus offers love to everyone (Mark 10:21 and John 11:3–5).
- Jesus forgives and doesn't judge (John 8:3–11).
- Jesus is never in a hurry (John 11:6).
- Jesus models right behavior for his disciples and followers (John 13:15).

By following these examples of Jesus, we can live as Jesus models for us and know that we are in him.

What can we do to be more like Jesus? What must we stop doing?

[Discover more about being an example in 1 Corinthians 11:1 and 1 Peter 2:21.]

Today's reading comes from *Love One Another: 40 Daily Reflections from the letters of 1, 2, and 3 John.*

DAY 8: HELP OTHERS
JOB 29

"I was like one who comforts mourners." (Job 29:25)

After Job gives his sarcastic retort to his lecturing friend, followed by his serious rebuttal, he pauses for a moment to collect his thoughts. Then he continues sharing the agony of his heart.

"Oh, how I wish life could return to how it once was, when the Almighty watched over me and blessed me. Those were the good old days. Now they're gone. I was in my prime then. My children surrounded me and filled me with joy. Prosperity abounded.

"Back then, people respected me. They made

way for me when I walked down the street, and they stopped talking to let me speak. They hung on my every word. Everyone had good things to say about me. They commended me for all the people I had helped: the poor, orphans, widows, the blind, the lame, the needy, those without an advocate, and victims of evil.

"I assumed I would die peacefully as an old man, living a comfortable life in my home. At my funeral, people would praise me. But that hope is now gone.

"Unlike you three, when I would speak people would listen. They'd let me have the final word. They would seek out my advice and take it all in. Whenever I smiled at someone, they couldn't believe I gave them my attention. I led them as a king leads his army. And I comforted them when they mourned, a lesson you should take to heart now."

Though now enduring difficulty, Job recalls how people used to commend him:

- Job helped the poor. He responded when people asked for assistance. It's easy to

Living a Faith that Matters

come to the aid of friends, but what about strangers?

- Job supported orphans. God has a special place in his heart for the parentless. When we befriend orphans, we benefit them and honor God too.
- Job brought joy to widows. God also wants to protect widows. Though their plight today isn't as detrimental as it was then, we must still help widows in need.
- Job did what was right. The Bible calls this righteousness. By right living, we set an example for others and honor God.
- Job pursued justice. The marginalized long for fair treatment. We can come to their defense.
- Job became eyes for the blind. We should assist those who can't see and strive to make their life a bit easier.
- Job became feet to those who couldn't walk. We can also aid those who struggle to get around.
- Job was a father to those in need. To people who lack the necessities of life, we can be like a loving, gracious parent to support them.

- Job was an advocate. We can stand up for the oppressed and work to find them relief.
- Job opposed evil. Sin is everywhere. Do we ignore it or fight it?
- Job rescued the victims. When evil exists, victims result. We can rescue them.

This list is long, overwhelming. Jesus said we'll always have the poor with us, but that fact isn't an excuse to ignore them. We should do what we can to assist those around us.

What can we do to help one person today? What need can we commit ourselves to address for the long term?

[Discover more about helping others in Matthew 5:42, Luke 18:22, and James 1:27.]

Today's reading comes from *Dear Theophilus Job: 40 Insights About Moving from Despair to Deliverance.*

DAY 9: LOVE YOUR NEIGHBOR
LUKE 10:25–37

"'Love the Lord your God with all your heart and with all your soul and with all your strength and with all your mind'; and, 'Love your neighbor as yourself.'" (Luke 10:27)

We call one of Jesus's more beloved teachings the Parable of the Good Samaritan. While the name for this parable comes from its main character, a better name is the Parable of Loving Your Neighbor.

Our story starts, like many of them do, with someone coming to Jesus to test him. The person is an expert in the law. Today we might call him a theologian. Let that sink in.

This person doesn't have a genuine question for

Jesus. Instead he seeks to make Jesus look bad and himself look good. Despite this, he poses a good question. He asks, "What must I do to receive life eternal?" Who doesn't want to know the answer to that?

As is often the case, Jesus responds to the question with another question. He asks the man, "What does the Law of Moses say about it?"

The theologian is ready with an answer. He says, "Love God totally, and then love your neighbor as much as you care for yourself."

"Correct," Jesus says. These two actions smartly summarize the Law of Moses. "Now, go do this and live."

The theologian squirms. He knows he falls short. He seeks a way out, a loophole to justify his unloving behavior. "Well," he says, "who is my neighbor, anyway?"

Jesus responds with his famous parable of The Good Samaritan. Here's a condensed version: a man gets beat up, robbed, and left to die. A priest—a religious VIP—walks by but doesn't check on the injured guy. A Levite—another religious person—passes by and doesn't help either. A Samaritan—a race despised by most Jews—sees the man and has compassion on him. At risk of also being robbed

Living a Faith that Matters

and beaten, the Samaritan invests his time and money to care for the injured man and make sure he'll be all right.

Then Jesus asks the theologian, "Which of these three men was a good neighbor?"

Unwilling to say "Samaritan" out loud, the theologian merely mumbles, "The one who showed mercy."

Jesus says, "Go and do the same."

The theologian must be in dismay. His plan backfired, and he's embarrassed.

Here are the key points.

First, Jesus confirms the way to eternal life is to love God and love our neighbors.

Second, the definition of neighbor is quite broad. It means everyone.

Third, the star of the story, the one with the right behavior, comes from a race the Jews look down on. He's an outsider, an outcast. The hero is a nobody. This should encourage everyone who doesn't fit in with religious institutions' or society's expectations. That means me, and it may mean you.

Is loving God and loving our neighbors enough to be right with God? How can we love our neighbors as God intends?

[Discover more about love in Leviticus 19:18, Deuteronomy 6:5, and 1 John 4:7–8.]

Today's reading comes from *Dear Theophilus: A 40-Day Devotional Exploring the Life of Jesus through the Gospel of Luke*.

DAY 10: LOVE ONE ANOTHER
1 JOHN 3:11–15

For this is the message you heard from the beginning: We should love one another. (1 John 3:11)

John tells his audience that we are to love one another.

It's not a new command but one we've heard from the beginning. He first mentions this in 1 John 2:7–8. And now he tells us what this command is: we are to love one another. It's that simple.

Saying that we've heard this from "the beginning" centers on Jesus.

When an expert in the law asks Jesus to name the greatest command, he says it's to love God.

Then he tacks on a second one—which makes it the second greatest command—to love others. In a most effective manner, these summarize everything in the Old Testament (Matthew 22:35–40).

We are to love God and love one another.

Jesus also talks about the importance of loving one another in his Sermon on the Mount. In that message he tells his listeners to love others in the same way that they love themselves (Matthew 7:12). He says the same thing, although more succinctly, in his Sermon on the Plain (Luke 6:31).

Though it's through Jesus that we get this essential command to love one another, we find it throughout the Old Testament. All the commands God gives his people either relate to their relationship with him or their relationship with others. As we've already mentioned, this comes from the Ten Commandments too. We first love God (commandments one through four) and then we love others (commandments five through ten).

This is why Jesus says the greatest command is to love God and the second greatest is to love others. Everything else in the Old Testament underscores these two (Matthew 22:37–40).

We find this command to love others hidden in the Levitical law too. Quoting the words of Father

God, Moses writes that we are to love our neighbors in the same way we love ourselves (Leviticus 19:18), which Jesus later quotes in Matthew 22:39.

Paul reiterates this in his letter to the church in Rome. He says we should owe no outstanding debt other than the continuing debt to love one another. When we do this, we fulfill the Old Testament commands (Romans 13:8).

In his letter to the church in Galatia, Paul confirms that we can keep the entire law by obeying the singular command to love our neighbor as much as we love ourselves (Galatians 5:14).

This command to love one another as we love ourselves is the essence of the Golden Rule. We are to treat others the way we want them to treat us. This means doing for them the same things that we'd like to receive ourselves. It also means not doing to them the things we don't want to receive. The Golden Rule is based on the Bible, going back to Leviticus 19:18.

This idea of loving one another as we love ourselves permeates Scripture. It's been there since the beginning.

What must we do differently to more fully obey God's essential command to love our neighbor? Beyond that, how well do we obey God's greatest command to love him?

[Discover more about John's instructions to love one another in John 13:34, John 13:35, 1 John 3:11, 1 John 3:23, 1 John 4:7, 1 John 4:11, 1 John 4:12, and 2 John 1:5.]

Today's reading comes from *Love One Another: 40 Daily Reflections from the letters of 1, 2, and 3 John.*

DAY 11: COUNT THE COST OF FOLLOWING JESUS
LUKE 14:25–35

"If anyone comes to me and does not hate father and mother, wife and children, brothers and sisters—yes, even their own life—such a person cannot be my disciple." (Luke 14:26)

On one of Jesus's travels, a large crowd trails behind him. He turns to them to talk about what it takes to truly follow him and be his disciple.

In doing so, Jesus uses some strong language. He uses the word hate.

He says that if we want to be his disciple—a true disciple—we must hate our parents, our spouse, our children, and our siblings. We must even hate our own life. Then he says we should pick up our cross and follow him.

What does he mean about picking up our cross? He's building upon his prior thought about hating our own life. In his day, prisoners dragged their cross through the city on their way to the execution site. For his followers to do this would confirm their allegiance to him and their willingness to die. That's commitment.

These are some serious barriers to deal with. Does Jesus really want us to hate our family and despise our own life to the point of death before we can fully follow him?

No.

Jesus uses exaggeration to make his point. He wants disciples who will make him their priority. He wants disciples to consider what it will cost to follow him. They must commit fully.

He shares two short parables to explain.

The first is a builder who wants to erect a tower. Before he starts, he figures out the total cost of the project. This will save him embarrassment from starting construction and not having enough money to finish. So, too, when we decide to follow Jesus.

The second is a king about to go into battle. Won't he first analyze the situation and look at troop strength to see if he can hope to defeat his enemy? And if he doesn't expect to win, wouldn't he pursue a peaceful solution instead of fighting?

Jesus doesn't want us to say we'll follow him and be his disciples if we don't really mean it, if we haven't considered what it will take to go all in for him. He's not trying to talk us out of it, but he wants us to contemplate what it may cost us to put him first in our lives. First over everything else.

Though we may say we put Jesus first, do our actions confirm it?

[Discover more about following Jesus in Luke 9:23 and Luke 9:57–62.]

Today's reading comes from *Dear Theophilus: A 40-Day Devotional Exploring the Life of Jesus through the Gospel of Luke*.

DAY 12: PROPHECY FULFILLED
ZECHARIAH 9–10

See, your king comes to you, righteous and victorious, lowly and riding on a donkey, on a colt, the foal of a donkey.
(Zechariah 9:9)

Babylon has conquered God's chosen people, deporting many of them. Those who remain in Jerusalem and throughout what's left of the nation of Judah struggle to eke out their survival. They're broken, abased, and vulnerable. They so need the Savior—whom the prophets foretold—to rescue them. So when Zechariah prophesies their King coming to them, they see this as reinforcing past prophecies. Their Savior will emerge as an answer to their prayers and the fulfillment of many predictions.

But their King doesn't come charging in on a stallion, armed for battle, and leading a mighty military force. He comes in humility, riding a donkey. This is a sign of peace. He comes in peace, and he will promote peace.

Though the people long for a physical savior, God will send them a spiritual Savior—which is far better.

Let's fast-forward to the New Testament and read about the fulfillment of Zechariah's prophecy. Matthew, Mark, and John all record this event in their biographies of Jesus. It happens on what we call Palm Sunday, a few days before Jesus's execution (Good Friday) and subsequent resurrection (Easter).

Here's what happens. As Jesus and his team walk toward Jerusalem, he sends two from his group to go on ahead to the village and look for a colt. They'll find the animal tied there, one that no one has ever ridden. They're to unfasten him and bring him to Jesus. If anyone asks what they're doing, they are to say, "The Lord needs to borrow him and will return him in a bit."

The pair do as Jesus instructed. And just as he

Living a Faith that Matters

said, they find the colt. When they untie him, some people question them, assuming they're thieves. But once the two disciples give Jesus's answer, the people let them go.

The pair bring the colt to Jesus and throw their coats onto the animal's back to provide a makeshift saddle. Jesus mounts the colt—remember, no one's ever ridden him before, so the animal's nature is to fight anyone who climbs on his back, but this doesn't happen. Jesus rides the animal into Jerusalem. And as he does, the people line the path, spreading their coats and palm branches out before him. They shout their praise to the Lord, acknowledging Jesus as their King. Lest we have any doubt, Matthew and John both note that this fulfills Zechariah's prediction.

This is just one of the awesome ways that Jesus accomplishes Old Testament prophecy.

Do we celebrate Jesus the way the people did on the first Palm Sunday? Are we in awe of how he fulfills what the prophets foretold?

[Discover more about the fulfillment of Zechariah's prophecy in Matthew 21:1–11, Mark 11:1–11, and John 12:12–19.]

Today's reading comes from *Dear Theophilus, Minor Prophets: 40 Prophetic Teachings about Unfaithfulness, Punishment, and Hope.*

DAY 13: JOB RESPONDS TO BILDAD
JOB 9–10

"If only there were someone to mediate between us, someone to bring us together, someone to remove God's rod from me, so that his terror would frighten me no more." (Job 9:33–34)

Bildad sits after lecturing Job, a pleased smirk playing on his lips. Job shakes his head and lowers his gaze, fixated on the heap of ashes before him. Bildad's words, too, fell short of the comfort that Job hoped his long-time friend would give. Instead, Bildad's monologue stirred frustration in Job's mind. Without looking up, Job speaks.

"I get what you're saying and agree with it to

some extent. But how can I, a mortal man whom God created, prove my innocence to him? He's God. I'm nobody. He's wise and powerful, controlling his creation with no effort. Who am I to him? I'm nothing. I can't defend myself, debate his decisions, or argue against his wisdom.

"I've done nothing wrong, but he doesn't care. Whether good or bad, we will all die. May my end come soon. If only there were someone to represent me to him, someone who could reconcile us and remove his punishment.

"I hate my life. I plead with the Almighty to give me a not guilty verdict. At least tell me what I've done wrong. As it is, he seems to delight in tormenting me, even though I'm innocent.

"He created me, so I suppose he can do whatever he wants. But does it make sense for him to destroy what he has made? I think not. If only I had died at birth, but here I am. As my life approaches its end, will he relent in his affliction of me—for but a moment—so that I may have one last taste of joy before I die?"

Though Bildad has provided Job with something to think about, it does nothing to ease Job's disquiet.

Living a Faith that Matters

Though Job maintains his innocence, he feels that God has punished him anyway, as though he's guilty. But who is Job to contend with God, to present his case so that he can vindicate himself?

We understand God as approachable. We know he wants us to live in community with him, but Job doesn't see this. Perhaps he can't.

Remember that Job wishes someone could come to mediate between him and God, someone who could bring them together, someone to remove God's punishment and take away Job's fear.

Jesus is that mediator for us. He gave his life for us to reconcile us with Papa, removing our punishment for our wrongdoing and taking away any fear we may have.

Do we see Jesus as our mediator? Have we accepted his work so that we may live in community with him?

[Discover more about Jesus as our mediator and Savior in John 14:6, Romans 8:38–39, Hebrews 9:15, and 1 Timothy 2:5.]

Today's reading comes from *Dear Theophilus Job: 40 Insights About Moving from Despair to Deliverance.*

DAY 14: JONAH'S CONFESSION
JONAH 1–2

*He answered, "I am a Hebrew and I worship the Lord, the God of heaven, who made the sea and the dry land." *(Jonah 1:9)

The story of Jonah is familiar to many people. God tells Jonah to go to Nineveh and deliver a harsh message to the people there. Jonah doesn't. He ignores God, jumps on a boat, and heads in the opposite direction from Nineveh. He wants to get as far away as possible from what God wants him to do.

God brews up a storm, buffeting the ship carrying Jonah. The sailors do all they can to keep their boat afloat, including pleading for protection from their gods, while an oblivious Jonah sleeps through everything. When the storm grows fierce, they wake Jonah and confront him. He confesses. He admits he's running from God, the God he worships, the God who created both land and sea.

Now the sailors really freak out.

Though Jonah says the only solution is to toss him into the deep, as a living sacrifice of sorts to the sea, the sailors redouble their efforts, so they won't be guilty of their passenger's death. But eventually they give up, asking God not to hold them accountable for Jonah's murder. They throw him into the sea, and the waves calm. They are safe and presume Jonah is dead.

God has other plans.

A huge fish swallows Jonah. He spends three days lodged in the fish's belly. From there he prays. He calls upon God, and God listens. Jonah wraps up his prayer praising God and with another confession. He affirms that salvation comes from God.

Then God has the fish deposit Jonah on dry land. This isn't a smooth exit. It's a violent expulsion. The fish vomits and Jonah ejects.

Living a Faith that Matters

There are similarities between Jonah and Jesus, but we must take care not to carry the comparison too far—for it will lead us astray. Jonah offers himself as a sacrifice to save the lives of the men on the ship. As good as dead, he spends three days in the belly of the fish. Then he emerges from his effective tomb when the fish deposits him on dry land.

In much grander fashion, Jesus later offers himself as a sacrifice to save the lives of everyone. He dies so that we may live. After spending three days in his tomb, he rises from the dead, proving that he has mastery over death.

In a simple way, this part of Jonah's life foreshadows what Jesus will do for all humanity. Jonah at first ran from his responsibility, but Jesus never wavered. Thank you, Jesus.

Are we running from God as Jonah first did, or are we embracing God through what Jesus did?

[Discover more about Jesus's sacrifice in Matthew 12:40 and Mark 8:31.]

Today's reading comes from *Dear Theophilus, Minor Prophets: 40 Prophetic Teachings about Unfaithfulness, Punishment, and Hope.*

DAY 15: BILDAD PROVIDES SOMETHING TO CONSIDER

JOB 25

"How then can a mortal be righteous before God?" (Job 25:4)

Just as Eliphaz has spoken three times to his friend Job, Bildad now takes his third turn. This time he doesn't bother to stand. Nor does he first glance at Eliphaz for approval to speak. Instead, Bildad looks at Job with a sad face and opens his mouth.

"God is in charge. Don't forget that. Who are we to understand him? We can't. His power is too great, his angels are too many, and his presence is everywhere.

"Can any of his mortal creation ever stand before him as good enough? Of course not! We were born in sin, and our sinful nature compels us to do what is wrong. We'll never be pure enough to approach him on our own. To him we are but a maggot, a mere worm."

Bildad draws in a slow and shallow breath, closes his eyes, and lowers his head.

In the shortest of all the speeches, Bildad gives Job—and us—something to think about. Between worshiping God for who he is and acknowledging that we are nothing next to him, Bildad asks an unsettling question: "How can a mere mortal be worthy to stand before God?"

It's a rhetorical question. We can't. We aren't good enough, and we never will be.

In the Old Testament, God gave his people the Law through Moses. The Law was a complex set of rules for proper worship and right living. It was also impossible for anyone to fully follow. Does that mean everyone in the Old Testament died separated from God? No. Scripture tells us that Abraham, for example, was justified (accepted) because of his faith in God.

Living a Faith that Matters

In the New Testament, we have Jesus. He fulfills the Old Testament Law, offering himself as the ultimate sacrifice to end all sacrifices and thereby removing from our permanent record all the mistakes we've ever made or will make. This makes us right with God and able to stand before him.

There's nothing we can do to earn our salvation or make us right with God. It's a matter of faith. Our right standing with God is a gift he offers to everyone. All we need to do is accept it.

Though we can, and should, strive to change our behavior *after* we've been made right with God through faith, we do this as a thank you note for what he has done. It's a response, not a requirement. Doing good isn't a condition to achieve something he offers us as a gift—for free—with no strings attached.

How do we view our relationship with God? Are we trying to earn a gift he's already offered to us?

[Discover more about doing good works, faith, and salvation in Ephesians 2:8–9.]

Today's reading comes from *Dear Theophilus Job: 40 Insights About Moving from Despair to Deliverance.*

DAY 16: JESUS IS THE WAY
JOHN 14:1–14

Jesus answered, "I am the way and the truth and the life."
(John 14:6)

Jesus has but a few hours left on earth. He wants to make the most of every moment. The teacher gives last-minute instructions to his disciples, trying to encourage them, which they'll need in the days, months, and years ahead. He talks about his father's house with many rooms, about him preparing a place for them, and about him coming back to get them so they can be with him. If this isn't cryptic enough, Jesus adds, "You know the way to where I'm going."

Thomas, one of Jesus's twelve disciples, doesn't. Speaking for the rest of them, he seeks clarification: "We don't know where you're going, so how can we know how to get there?"

Jesus gives him a five-part answer, which John records for us. Jesus says, "I am the way and the truth and the life. No one comes to the Father except through me."

Let's explore this.

First, Jesus opens with, "I am." Don't miss this. In the Old Testament, God the Father tells Moses to think of him as *I am* (Exodus 3:13–14). When Jesus repeats this phrase in his concise answer, it's intentional. We're reminded that Jesus also exists as God, as God the Son. Jesus is the *I am*, just as much as the Father.

Next, Jesus gives the first of three instructive phrases, saying that he is "the way." Jesus himself serves as the path to God the Father. As our Messiah, he points us in the right direction. He provides the means for us to get there. Soon he'll do this by serving as the ultimate sin sacrifice for all of humanity, past, present, and future.

Jesus adds that he is "the truth." He personifies what is real. He exemplifies truth, proclaims truth,

Living a Faith that Matters

and models truth. We can always rely on the words of Jesus as dependable. His words will set us free (John 8:31–32).

After confirming that he is the way and the truth, he adds that he is "the life." Not only does Jesus give us life, but he *is* life. After giving us life at creation, he continues as one who lives forever. We, as his followers, will enjoy eternity with him.

The final of the five key phrases in this verse is "through me." Jesus is the door to Father God. The first four parts of Jesus's answer culminate in his conclusion: through him we reconcile with God the Father, our spiritual Papa.

Jesus supplies what we need for our journey in this life and into the next. He is the source of life, of truth, and of the way to the Father.

Do we trust Jesus to be the way, the truth, and the life? What does this mean to us? How does this influence how we live our life?

[Discover more about Jesus being truth and life in Luke 20:21, John 11:25, and John 18:37.]

Today's reading comes from *Living Water: 40 Reflections on Jesus's Life and Love from the Gospel of John.*

DAY 17: WE ARE ON THE WINNING SIDE
JOHN 16:16–33

"Take heart! I have overcome the world." (John 16:33)

As Jesus continues his last instructions to his disciples, he talks of his departure, which his disciples will mourn, and the world will celebrate. But as a woman struggles through childbirth, and then rejoices over the birth of her baby, so too the disciples' grief will turn into joy. Jesus will see them again, which means they'll see him again. No one will be able to steal their joy in Jesus. He continues to offer encouragement, mentioning answered prayer and Father God's love for them.

The disciples start to understand. At last, they

believe. This is a good thing because he has little time left to explain, so they better understand now.

He affirms their belief in him and warns they'll soon scatter, each retreating to his own home. Though they will leave him, Jesus won't be alone. His Father will stay.

Jesus says he's telling them these things to give them peace. And even though the world will pile trouble upon them, "Don't worry," Jesus says, "I have overcome the world."

Jesus wants them not to worry but to overflow with peace. By extension, he tells us the same.

Worry occurs when we look at our life from a human perspective. We see threats all around us, we feel the burden of living for Jesus in a world that is against him, and we combat an enemy set on causing us pain. These worries can weigh us down and rob us of our peace.

Yet, through God's perspective, we can see through fresh eyes. We know how the story ends. We know that Jesus, through his ultimate sacrifice, has forgiven our sins and defeated the evil one. He has overcome. Though we may not realize the full release that his victory gives us now, we will experience it completely as we persist in following him and being his disciple. This should fill us with peace.

Since Jesus has overcome the world, if we believe in him and follow him, we, too, can overcome our world through him. If we align with Jesus, we are on the winning side.

Are we winning through Jesus? How does knowing that Jesus overcame the world guide our attitudes and actions?

[Discover what else John says about overcoming the world and the evil one in 1 John 2:13–14, 4:4, and 5:1–5.]

Today's reading comes from *Living Water: 40 Reflections on Jesus's Life and Love from the Gospel of John*.

DAY 18: THE FINAL SACRIFICE
HEBREWS 9:16–28

Christ was sacrificed once to take away the sins of many; and he will appear a second time, not to bear sin, but to bring salvation. (Hebrews 9:28)

We're not wrong to consider a covenant like a will. A will doesn't go into effect until after death occurs. Under the old covenant this was the death of an animal. Under Jesus's new covenant it is *his* death. In both cases, death sets in motion what each covenant specifies.

As the old covenant requires the spilling of blood, so too does the new one. Though the old covenant demands an annual blood sacrifice of animals, the new covenant does not. As the perfect human sacrifice, Jesus's death ends the need for ongoing animal sacrifices that only temporarily cleanse the people of their sins.

The writers of Hebrews remind us that Jesus doesn't enter the earthly replica of the tabernacle when he dies. Instead, he enters heaven itself, into God's very presence. In addition, Jesus doesn't need to do this over and over, as did the high priests under the old covenant. Jesus suffers and dies one time. Once is enough. Jesus's death is the final sacrifice to remove the sins of all people throughout all time.

In this way Jesus comes to earth to die once, removing the sins of many. And he will appear a second time, not to die again, but to bring salvation to those who await him with expectation.

We can interpret this second appearance of Jesus in multiple ways. Here are two thoughts.

Just as he ascended into heaven after he rose from the dead, he will one day descend from heaven and return to earth (Acts 1:10–11). Then he will gather his followers and take them to be with him forever (John 14:2–3).

This will complete his saving work. This promise, however, doesn't apply to every believer but only

Living a Faith that Matters

to those living when he returns. Those who died prior to his second coming will already be with him.

Another understanding of his second appearance is to compare this with the high priests' annual duty under the old covenant. The people see the high priest enter the Most Holy Place to offer the annual sacrifice. But they can't see what he's doing. They don't know when he finishes.

Instead, they wait outside for the high priest to emerge from the Most Holy Place. Only when they see him a second time do they know the sacrifice has been completed. Then they can have assurance their sins are covered—for one more year.

In the same way as these Old Testament high priests, Jesus appears the second time to confirm the sacrifice has been completed. His death represents the final sacrifice, the sacrifice to end them all.

Though this second explanation may not mean much to us today, the Hebrew people of old—the recipients of the letter to the Hebrews—would have certainly grasped the connection. It would comfort them, tying the old covenant that they know well with Jesus's new covenant that they're just beginning to embrace.

Are we awaiting Jesus's return with eager expectation? What will he find us doing when he returns a second time?

[Discover a parallel story about another priest serving in the temple—offering the daily burning of incense—in Luke 1:8–22.]

Today's reading comes from *Run with Perseverance: A 40-Day Devotional Bible Study on the Book of Hebrews about Faith and Godly Living.*

DAY 19: WAIT FOR IT
ACTS 1:1–8

"Do not leave Jerusalem, but wait for the gift my Father promised, which you have heard me speak about." (Acts 1:4)

Acts picks up where the book of Luke ended. As with many sequels, Acts opens with a review of what happened in the first book. Again addressing Theophilus, Luke references his first letter, which we call Luke, the third book in the New Testament.

Here's the recap: In the forty days between Jesus's resurrection and his return to heaven, he appears to his followers many times. He proves he's alive and reminds them about the kingdom of God. Slowly, things begin to click for them. Jesus isn't a military leader who will overthrow the Roman rule. He's a spiritual revolutionary to fulfill God's plan for humanity, set in motion before time began.

Finally, Jesus's teaching starts to take on new meaning. The misconceptions of his followers' prior thinking fall away. But it takes time to reorient their perspective from the physical world to a spiritual reality. When one of his followers asks if Jesus is ready to restore Israel as a nation, his answer is "not now." The timing is secret.

Instead, Jesus tells his followers to wait.

Waiting is counter to our modern-day thinking. Delay represents lost opportunity. We must maintain momentum to propel our cause forward. Yet Jesus says, "Wait." It seems ill-advised. However, much of what Jesus says is contrary to human wisdom. We should expect the unexpected from Jesus. If he says to wait, this shouldn't cause dismay. Sometimes inaction is the best action—especially when God says to delay.

From a human perspective, they should organize, plan, and deploy across the region to tell others about Jesus. They have experience going out two-by-two. Jesus trained them to do just that. They seem ready, but Jesus says to wait.

Wait for a special gift promised by Papa: a new

kind of baptism, a supernatural anointing. While John uses water, this new baptism will be with the Holy Spirit. The Holy Spirit will empower them to tell others about Jesus.

This new baptism doesn't have the tangible use of water but the intangible power of Spirit. Yet the two are connected, for the Holy Spirit shows up when John baptizes Jesus with water.

Consider John's baptism. He lowers people into the water, submerges them, and lifts them out. John's baptism symbolically parallels death, burial, and resurrection. Cleansing takes place. It's a powerful, beautiful imagery.

When Jesus emerges from the waters of his baptism, heaven opens and the Holy Spirit, in a visible form that resembles a dove, comes upon him. God's voice booms. He confirms Jesus as his son, whom he loves and whose actions he affirms. In this case, Jesus's water baptism links to the Holy Spirit. This foreshadows what is to come for his disciples with the promised gift of the Holy Spirit.

While different streams of Christianity explain the Holy Spirit's work in different ways, with varying present-day implications, we should use what happened then to inform our understanding and practices now.

Do we need to reconsider the role of the Holy Spirit in our life and our church to better align with the Bible?

[Discover more about the Holy Spirit in Acts 2:38, Acts 10:44–45, Acts 11:15–16, Acts 19:2–6, Romans 15:13, 1 Corinthians 6:19, and Jude 1:20–21.]

Today's reading comes from *Dear Theophilus, Acts: 40 Devotional Insights for Today's Church*.

DAY 20: A NEW COVENANT
HEBREWS 8:1–6

The ministry Jesus has received is as superior to theirs as the covenant of which he is mediator is superior to the old one.
(Hebrews 8:6)

Hebrews 7 explains about the need for a new priesthood to replace the old one, one which the Hebrew people are most familiar with. Lest there be any doubt, Jesus is this new high priest. But unlike all those high priests who descended from Aaron and preceded him Jesus as our high priest is unique.

After his resurrection from the dead, Jesus ascends into heaven. He sits at the right hand of the

Father's throne. There, Jesus serves in the heavenly sanctuary—the true tabernacle. God himself established this supernatural temple, one far superior to the one built on earth by human hands.

This tabernacle here on earth, along with the temple that replaced it, serves as mere copies of the original one in heaven, a shadow of what exists in the supernatural realm. Though the heavenly version far exceeds its earthly counterpart, the two parallel each other, with the earthly one revealing truth to us about the heavenly one.

We get a sense of the importance of their similarity because God warned Moses to build the tabernacle exactly how the Almighty had instructed his servant (Exodus 25:40). This occurred when Moses went up Mount Sinai and spent forty days with God to receive detailed instructions about the tabernacle, worship, and right living (Exodus 24–31).

If it's critical for the construction of the tabernacle on earth to match what is in heaven, there must be a reason for it.

I sense the earthly tabernacle/temple is connected to the supernatural one in heaven, linking the two together. When Jesus dies and the veil in the temple tears in half here on earth, I envision the corresponding veil in the heavenly counterpart simultaneously rending. On earth this symbolically shows we have direct access to God in the Most Holy Place, whereas in heaven our access is tangible to the very throne of God and his presence. This, of course, is merely how I envision it.

Returning to today's text, this discussion about the earthly tabernacle mimicking the superior one in heaven, shows that Jesus's ministry is in the same way superior to the priesthood of the Old Testament. It also shows us that the new covenant through Jesus, which he mediates, is likewise superior to the old one.

This is because the new covenant offers us better promises. It pledges to give us the forgiveness of sin and life eternal with God in heaven.

In what other ways might it be important for the earthly tabernacle to match the model in heaven? How is Jesus's ministry superior to that of the Old Testament high priests?

[Discover more about the tabernacle in Acts 7:44–50 and Revelation 15:5.]

Today's reading comes from *Run with Perseverance: A 40-Day Devotional Bible Study on the Book of Hebrews about Faith and Godly Living.*

DAY 21: CONFESS OUR SINS
1 JOHN 1:8–10

If we confess our sins, he is faithful and just and will forgive us our sins and purify us from all unrighteousness. (1 John 1:9)

As a young teen, I had a Sunday school teacher who claimed he sometimes would go an entire day without sinning. Granted, he didn't claim to be without sin, only that he had some days where he avoided it.

Though he was a godly man and I respected him deeply, I questioned if such a thing were possible. At least I doubted it was for me. It could be I was too sensitive to sin or wrongly confused temptation with sin, but I wondered if I could even go one hour without sinning, let alone twenty-four.

Today's trio of verses addresses sin and our attitude toward it. This passage opens and closes with parallel verses that restate the same idea: if we claim to live a life without sin, we delude ourselves. (My teacher only claimed to be sinless for a day, not a lifetime.)

Scripture says that everyone has sinned and falls short of God's expectations (Romans 3:23). Therefore, if we claim we're sinless, we make God out to be a liar and do not accept his truth.

Fortunately, we don't need to wallow in our sinfulness. Sandwiched between these two verses about our sin-filled nature, we find a most encouraging promise.

John says if we confess our sins, God will forgive them, purifying us from our unrighteousness, that is, from our wrong behavior. We can count on it.

John also writes that Jesus died for the sins of the entire world (1 John 2:2), but we don't automatically receive his forgiveness. Through this sacrificial death, Jesus has prepared the gift of salvation for everyone. But until we receive his present it's not ours.

We can receive Jesus's gift of salvation when we

admit our faults. But to do that, we must first acknowledge that our sins need forgiving.

When we confess our sins, that is, admit our faults to Jesus, we can have confidence in his response of forgiveness. This is because he's already died for our sins to make us right with Father God. He will be faithful to forgive. And his forgiveness is because his death satisfied what justice demands. This is what it means when John writes that Jesus is faithful and just.

When we confess our sins, we will receive his forgiveness. This purifies us from all the wrongs we have done and all the wrong things we will do.

Have we confessed our sins to Jesus and received his forgiveness? How should we live our life knowing that he has purified us from our unrighteousness?

[Discover more about confession in Psalm 32:5, Proverbs 28:13, and Acts 19:18.]

Today's reading comes from *Love One Another: 40 Daily Reflections from the letters of 1, 2, and 3 John.*

DAY 22: GOD'S NEW CREATION
2 CORINTHIANS 5:11–6:2

Therefore, if anyone is in Christ, the new creation has come: The old has gone, the new is here! (2 Corinthians 5:17)

The biblical account starts with our creation in Genesis 1 and 2. After each stage of his handiwork, God proclaims the results as "good." On day six, when he fashions people—male and female, created in his image—he surveys all that he has made, and this time pronounces it as "very good" (Genesis 1:31).

Yet it may not be good enough. Here's why. In Jesus and through Jesus we can become a *new* creation, implicitly better than God's original version. If the Genesis creation was very good, what does that make us as his new creation through Jesus? How about exceptionally good?

To become God's new creation, we must believe in and follow Jesus. This transitions us from God's original creation into his new creation. But there's more. As God's new creation in Christ, the old way disappears, and a new perspective emerges. This marks our spiritual transformation.

Paul understands this well. He made a significant transformation from his old approach of harassing, hunting, and killing Jesus's followers. Replacing this he becomes a zealous follower of Christ, who endures much to encounter, convert, and instruct people about salvation through Jesus.

Like Paul, as a new creation in Jesus, our old approach to living goes away. We no longer find ourselves enslaved to sin. Though evil and the temptation to do wrong still surround us, we now comprehend them from a new perspective, one we receive in Christ and through Christ. Day by day we persevere in becoming this new creation through Jesus. We move toward perfection.

The Old Testament recognizes humanity's sins and prescribes a lengthy set of rules of what to do and not do. Yet no one can completely follow these commands. If we stumble just once, we're as guilty as if we fail every time (James 2:10).

The Old Testament ordered recurring animal sacrifices as sin offerings to address the people's shortcomings. In the New Testament, Jesus comes to fulfill the Old Testament's way. He becomes the ultimate sacrifice, the once-and-for-all payment for all sins throughout all time. Through him we can become a new creation; the old system disappears, replaced by Jesus's fresh approach.

This makes us God's new creation.

How does being a new creation in Christ affect how we live? Do our actions and attitudes prove we really believe the old is gone, and the new has come?

[Discover more about creation in Romans 1:20, Romans 8:22, Galatians 6:15, and Ephesians 1:4.]

Today's reading comes from *Love Is Patient: 40 Devotional Gems and Bible Study Truths from Paul's Letters to the Corinthians.*

DAY 23: DEALING WITH THEOLOGICAL DISAGREEMENTS
ACTS 15:1–35

Then some of the believers who belonged to the party of the Pharisees stood up and said, "The Gentiles must be circumcised and required to keep the law of Moses." (Acts 15:5)

Until now, the church has enjoyed much unity. They've gotten along, just as Jesus prayed they would. And they quickly resolved the one small, potentially divisive issue that arose about food distribution. Now they face a more challenging issue: theological disagreement. Will they overcome it, or will it cause division?

Some people from Judea show up at Antioch.

Luke doesn't tell us who these people are, and it's just as well that we don't know. They insist that the path to Jesus must be through Judaism. They specifically require the circumcision of converts, as commanded in the Law of Moses.

This isn't the first time the circumcision issue has come up. In Acts 11:1–18, this issue arose, and the church dealt with it quickly. The result was a consensus that Gentiles can be part of the church and don't have to undergo the Jewish rite of circumcision.

However, it seems that not everyone is aware of this decision, or at least they don't care about it. Some of the Pharisees who follow Jesus insist that Gentiles who want to join them must undergo circumcision and keep the Law of Moses.

The church leaders in Jerusalem get together to consider this issue—again.

Peter reminds them of his experience at Cornelius's house, when the Holy Spirit came upon the Gentiles there. As non-Jews, they weren't circumcised, and no one required them to undergo this ritual. Nor did they have to follow Jewish law. The simple requirement was that they believe in Jesus and follow him.

Then Barnabas and Paul share their experience working with Gentiles and all the supernatural things God did to bring these people into his church.

Next James, likely the brother of Jesus, speaks. He quotes the prophecy of Amos who predicted that even Gentiles would turn to God. James then summarizes his perspective that the church shouldn't add any unnecessary roadblocks for the Gentiles who want to follow Jesus.

The elders, along with the whole church, agree with James's recommendation. They draft a letter outlining their conclusion. Paul and Barnabas, accompanied by Judas (also called Barsabbas) and Silas, deliver the letter to the church in Antioch. This good news encourages the people. Judas and Silas stick around a while to help the church grow in their faith. Then they return to Jerusalem, leaving Paul and Barnabas to continue the work in Antioch.

When theological disagreements arise, do we allow them to divide us, or do we seek consensus to stay united?

[Discover more about Amos's prophecy in Amos 9:11–12.]

Today's reading comes from *Dear Theophilus, Acts: 40 Devotional Insights for Today's Church*.

DAY 24: NO DIVISIONS
1 CORINTHIANS 1:1–17

That all of you agree with one another in what you say and that there be no divisions among you, but that you be perfectly united in mind and thought. (1 Corinthians 1:10)

Paul wants the Corinthians to function as one and to live in unity—of like mind. But this unity isn't just a message for them because Paul also encourages the churches in Ephesus, Philippi, and Colossae to pursue unity with other believers. In the same way, Jesus prayed that we—his future followers—would live as one, just as he and his Father exist as one (John 17:21).

But to our shame, we divide Jesus's church. We

live in disharmony. We fight with each other over our traditions and our practices and how we comprehend God.

We spar over worship style, song selection, and a myriad of other things that relate to church practices and our perception of right living. Or to avoid these errors, we simply ignore those with other perspectives, and that's just as bad.

But the world watches us. They judge Jesus through our actions. They test what we say by the things we do. And we often fail their test.

With our words we talk about how Jesus loves everyone, but with our deeds we diminish our brothers and sisters in Christ with a holier-than-thou discord. If we can't love those in the church, how can we hope to love those outside it? We can't.

It's no wonder the world no longer respects the church of Jesus and is quick to dismiss his followers as hypocritical zealots. We brought it upon ourselves with our church splits and tens of thousands of Protestant denominations, resulting from our petty arguments over practices and theology and everything in between.

In the face of a couple of billion Christians, mostly living life contrary to God's will by not getting along with each other, what can you and I do to correct this error?

We can change this one person at a time. Find another Christian who goes to a church radically different from yours (or has dropped out of church) and embrace them as one in Christ.

If you are a mainline Christian, find a charismatic follower of Jesus and get to know him or her. If all your friends are Protestants, go to Mass and make some new friends.

If all the Christians you know look just like you, think like you, and act like you, find another Christian who is not like you. Diversify your Christian relationships to expand your understanding of what following Jesus truly looks like.

In Jesus, we are the same. It's time we embrace one another. The world is watching us to discover what we do. Instead of seeing our selfishness and sins, may they see Jesus instead.

What can we do to better live in unity with other Christians? What action can we take today?

[Discover more about unity through Jesus in Ephesians 4:3 and Philippians 4:2–3.]

Today's reading comes from *Love Is Patient: 40 Devotional Gems and Bible Study Truths from Paul's Letters to the Corinthians.*

DAY 25: RUN WITH PERSEVERANCE
HEBREWS 12:1–3

Let us run with perseverance the race marked out for us, fixing our eyes on Jesus, the pioneer and perfecter of faith.
(Hebrews 12:1–2)

Today's passage opens with the word *therefore*. *Therefore* connects what follows it with what precedes it. In this case it's our Hebrews 11 hall of faith.

It provides us with the imagery of a great cloud of witnesses surrounding us, people of noteworthy faith. We can interpret their witness in two ways. One is that their lives serve as a witness to us. The other is that they are witnessing *our* lives. Imagine these Old Testament Saints watching us and cheering us on as we move down our journey of faith. It's a heady thought. May we find encouragement in it.

Because of their example and their witness, the writers of Hebrews encourage us to do two things. Both begin with the inspiring instruction of "let us."

First, the text says to let us throw off everything that holds us back, to jettison each weight that slows us down. This includes the entanglement of sin. If we wrongly hold on to these things, it does not negate our right standing with Jesus, but it does affect how we live our lives while we're here on earth and the reward we'll receive once we leave this place. Remember, we have an impressive throng of witnesses cheering us on.

Second, let us run with perseverance the race before us. Having ridden ourselves of all the baggage that would slow us down, we're ready to run. We are poised to speed down the path God has for us. As we do, we want to keep our focus on Jesus, to maintain a steady gaze on him. He is the reason for our faith and the perfecter of it.

Jesus now sits in heaven at God's right hand. He, too, is our witness. His life and sacrifice serve as a witness to us. And, from the vantage of heaven,

Living a Faith that Matters

he witnesses what we're doing with this new life that he gave us.

If the patriarchs' witness motivates us to move forward in faith, how much more should Jesus's witness? He endured for us, which should encourage us to persevere for him, to not grow weary or lose heart.

We must, therefore, run our race with perseverance.

How can we best run our race with perseverance? How can Jesus and the great cloud of witnesses encourage us in our faith journey?

[Discover more about perseverance in Romans 5:1–4, James 1:2–4, and 2 Peter 1:5–7.]

Today's reading comes from *Run with Perseverance: A 40-Day Devotional Bible Study on the Book of Hebrews about Faith and Godly Living.*

DAY 26: DEVOTED TO JESUS
2 CORINTHIANS 11:1–33

But I am afraid that just as Eve was deceived by the serpent's cunning, your minds may somehow be led astray from your sincere and pure devotion to Christ. (2 Corinthians 11:3)

In 1 Corinthians 15:22 we see Paul placing the blame for humanity's fall on Adam. In the above passage, however, Paul focuses on Eve's role in the couple's disobedience to their creator's command. He says plainly that the serpent's cunning deceived Eve.

Paul worries that in the same way the church in Corinth might also diverge from their faith—that they'll go astray by following the wrong influences of others, thereby ditching their devotion to Jesus.

He doesn't share the source of this deception. But the threat could arise from false teachers who misrepresent Jesus, the devil's cunning schemes, or both.

Paul fears this outcome for the church in Corinth. This is despite the eighteen months he spent with them, a subsequent visit, his prayers, and his letters of instruction to them. He has invested much into them, yet he's afraid they'll veer off track. If, after all this, Paul carries this unease about them, we too should guard against influences that could lead us astray.

This isn't an issue of them walking away from their faith. Instead, Paul is concerned that these negative influences will detract from their "sincere and pure devotion" to Jesus.

The word devotion only occurs one other time in the New Testament. You might already suspect where. It appears in Paul's other letter to his friends in Corinth. This time he urges them to live with an "undivided devotion to the Lord" (1 Corinthians 7:35).

Merging these two related verses, we get a sense that our devotion to Jesus should be sincere, pure, and undivided. The opposite of this is insincere, impure, and divided. This gives us a sense of incomplete devotion, a partial commitment to following Jesus. It's unacceptable.

When we believe in Jesus and follow him, he wants us to go all in. There is no looking back (Genesis 19:23–26 and Luke 9:62). God deserves our complete devotion for the rest of our lives. We must reject anything or anyone that distracts us from him.

Are we fully devoted to Jesus, or only partially so? What influences must we remove from our life that threaten to distract us from our dedication to our Savior?

[Discover more about devotion to Jesus in Matthew 6:24, Hebrews 10:36–39, and 1 John 1:6–7.]

Today's reading comes from *Love Is Patient: 40 Devotional Gems and Bible Study Truths from Paul's Letters to the Corinthians.*

DAY 27: HOLY SPIRIT POWER
ACTS 19:1 TO ACTS 20:1

When Paul placed his hands on them, the Holy Spirit came on them, and they spoke in tongues and prophesied. (Acts 19:6)

On his missionary journey, Paul heads to Ephesus. He finds a dozen believers there but is shocked that they haven't received the gift of the Holy Spirit. In fact, they don't even know who the Holy Spirit is. Paul probes a little deeper. "What baptism did you receive?"

"John's."

Paul explains that John's baptism is for repentance, preparing the way for Jesus.

Upon hearing this, the disciples want to be baptized in Jesus's name. After they are, Paul places his hands on them, and the Holy Spirit fills them. They speak in tongues and prophesy.

Next, Paul goes to the synagogue to tell his fellow Jews about Jesus, but they refuse to believe. They oppose Paul and speak against Team Jesus. Paul leaves the synagogue, taking the disciples with him. They have daily discussions in Tyrannus's lecture hall. This goes on for two years. Eventually everyone in the area hears about Jesus.

Just as the people sought healing by having Peter's shadow fall on them, God does amazing miracles through Paul too. He touches cloths, such as handkerchiefs and aprons, imparting supernatural power into them. They're taken to the sick, who are healed from their diseases, and those with evil spirits are freed.

Jesus said his followers would do even greater things than he had done once he returned to his Father. We certainly see this in Paul, as well as Peter before him.

In this new thing that God is doing in Jesus's church, we see the Holy Spirit take a central role. Holy Spirit power fills the people. The afflicted

Living a Faith that Matters

receive healing, and evil spirits are exorcised in Jesus's name. The supernatural abounds.

Some Jews invoke the name of Jesus, who Paul talks about, to cast out evil spirits. The seven sons of Sceva try this too. They don't know what they're doing. It's more supernatural power than they can handle. It backfires.

One day the evil spirit doesn't obey them. Instead, it talks back. "I know Jesus. And I know Paul. But who do you think you are?" Then the possessed man jumps them and beats all seven brothers. They run away bleeding and naked.

As word of what happened to these brothers spreads, a holy fear fills the people. They revere the name of Jesus. Many believers confess their sins. Some of those involved in sorcery show their repentance by burning all their scrolls.

Demetrius is one of the locals who opposes Paul. Though Demetrius claims this is for religious reasons, it's economic. He stirs up the people and a mob forms. After the city clerk quiets the uprising, Paul encourages the disciples, says goodbye, and leaves town.

The early church moved in supernatural power through the Holy Spirit. What can we apply from that in today's church?

[Discover more about Jesus's promise to his disciples —and us—in John 14:12–14.]

Today's reading comes from *Dear Theophilus, Acts: 40 Devotional Insights for Today's Church*.

DAY 28: THE REVELATION OF JESUS
REVELATION 1:1–3

The revelation from Jesus Christ, which God gave him to show his servants what must soon take place. (Revelation 1:1)

We think of the book of Revelation as John's revelation, but, in fact, it is Jesus's. John is only the recipient. This revelation comes from Jesus. Father God gave it to him. Jesus shares this revelation with John through a supernatural vision as the apostle communes with God in the spiritual realm (Revelation 1:10).

An angel shows up in John's vision to reveal Jesus's revelation. The intent of the vision—that is, the revelation—is to show John what will soon take place.

As we comprehend time, we can easily conclude that *soon* has already occurred, since we are now 2,000 years distant from John's recording of these words. Yet we must acknowledge that God views time differently than we do. A thousand years to us are but a day to him and a day to us may be a thousand years to him (Psalm 90:4 and 2 Peter 3:8).

So when we read John's words that the time is near, this shouldn't perplex us. If we literally equate 2,000 years of our time to two days for God, then we are but two days removed from this revelation. In this respect, we can accept that the time is, indeed, quite near.

Yet a literal application of Scripture's statement about God's view of time may be an overreach. The principle to grasp, however, is that we comprehend time much differently than God. Given this, we can accept that these events will soon take place because the time is near, even though those words took place two millennia ago. Time isn't a problem for God, only for us.

John confirms that his vision is a prophecy. In a delightful simplicity, we'll receive God's blessing by

Living a Faith that Matters

merely reading it, hearing it, and taking it to heart (Revelation 1:3). Don't miss this point.

John doesn't say we need to understand what it says. Just like the rest of Scripture, we can now only know in part. Rather, we should read it and be amazed. That's the intent. And God will bless us when we do.

Beyond that we find another hint at the purpose of John's vision much later in Revelation. The aim of Revelation may be simply to worship God and celebrate Jesus (Revelation 19:10).

How well do we accept that we understand time differently than God? How content are we to read, hear, and take to heart the book of Revelation?

[Discover what else John says about Jesus and how it relates to our view of time in John 1:1–5.]

Today's reading comes from *A New Heaven and a New Earth: 40 Practical Insights from John's Book of Revelation.*

DAY 29: THE ALPHA AND OMEGA
REVELATION 22:12–16

"I am the Alpha and the Omega, the First and the Last, the Beginning and the End." (Revelation 22:13)

This passage in Revelation records Jesus's words, and it's his final teaching in the Bible. As such, it deserves our careful attention.

Jesus comes with his reward, to give each person what they deserve based on what they've done. This comes as a surprising declaration, implying that we'll receive salvation through our actions.

Aren't we saved by grace through faith? Yes, we are. Isn't salvation a gift that we can't earn? Yes, it is (Ephesians 2:8–9).

Then why will Jesus look at what we've done? Though we may remember our many sins and cringe with shame at the recollection, God blots out the sins of those who follow him, remembering them no more (Isaiah 43:25). Through him we have a clean slate.

This means that God's record of what we've done is far different than our own recollection. To him we are his pure, spotless bride (Ephesians 5:27). When we follow Jesus, we need not wallow in worry over our past mistakes because through him we are made right (Romans 5:19).

This restored standing gives us the right to eat from the tree of life. We may enter the new Jerusalem through the city gates where we'll become Jesus's bride. Nothing impure will be able to enter (Revelation 21:27).

Yet not all will have this confidence when they see Jesus coming at the end of time. He says that the practitioners of magic arts, the sexually immoral, murderers, and idolaters, along with all who persist in lying will remain on the outside looking in. He'll bar their entrance into the new Jerusalem.

Does this list sound familiar?

Living a Faith that Matters

God gave a similar itemization in Revelation 21. God's list is a bit longer, but he includes everything Jesus mentions. The people who do these things will end up in the fiery lake that burns with sulfur. This is the second death (Revelation 21:8).

In his message, Jesus also reveals some names for himself. He is the Root of David, as well as his Offspring, both preceding and following Israel's second king. Jesus is the bright Morning Star. And Jesus is the Alpha and the Omega. That is, he is the First and the Last, the Beginning and the End.

This is a reminder that just as Jesus is present here in Revelation at the end of time, he was also present at the beginning of creation (Genesis 1:26 and John 1:1–4). Through him we are, and through him we will be. He created our physical bodies, and he saves our spiritual selves.

Are we still holding on to the sins that Jesus has already forgiven and forgotten? How can we better respond to Jesus as the Alpha and Omega?

[Discover more about the Alpha and Omega, the First and the Last, in Revelation 1:8, 1:17, 2:8, and

21:6. Read more about the morning star in 2 Peter 1:19 and Revelation 2:28.]

Today's reading comes from *A New Heaven and a New Earth: 40 Practical Insights from John's Book of Revelation.*

DAY 30: COMING SOON
REVELATION 22:17–21

He who testifies to these things says, "Yes, I am coming soon." (Revelation 22:20)

After Jesus finishes his last teaching in the book of Revelation, the Holy Spirit weighs in as well. But it's not just him. It's also the bride (not the bridegroom). This means you and me, all whose names appear in the Lamb's book of life. We join with the Holy Spirit to bid people to "Come!" And everyone who hears our offer we'll add to the invitation and likewise say to others, "Come!"

This invite is to anyone who's thirsty. They may come to him. Anyone who wants to can receive

Jesus's no-strings-attached gift of living water. Isn't this exciting?

Only a few verses ago, in Revelation 22:11, it seemed too late for those who hadn't already decided to follow Jesus. But now it feels as though they're given one last, final chance. The invitation, given three times, is to come to Jesus and receive the water of life.

We serve a God of second chances. And third chances. And even more than we can count. He is patient because he wants as many to come to him as possible (2 Peter 3:9).

But we need to come to Jesus before it's too late, perhaps before he returns, which will happen soon.

In this chapter in Revelation, Jesus speaks three times.

The first is in verse 7. Then comes his longer message (which we just covered) in verses 12 through 16. His final words in all of Scripture appear at the end of verse 20.

In each of these three passages he repeats the same phrase: "I am coming soon."

This threefold testimony from Jesus that he's coming soon repeats to underscore its importance. Though Jesus saying it once is enough, saying it

Living a Faith that Matters

twice adds emphasis, while three times confirms beyond all doubt that it will happen.

Yet we must acknowledge that God reckons time differently than we do. What is *soon* to him may not be *soon* to us. Indeed, 2,000 years ago Jesus told his followers that his kingdom was near, that it was coming soon. The early church understood this as meaning any day, just as many people now make the same assumption.

As Jesus's followers, how can we understand his promise that he is coming soon? How should we live our lives in this tension between him coming soon and having already waited two millennia?

We must embrace both scenarios.

We should strive to simultaneously expect that he's coming back today and seek to live every day for the rest of our lives to advance his kingdom and raise up future generations to follow him too. We should balance the seemingly competing realities that he is coming soon *and* that we may die before he does.

Since Jesus could come any day, what are we doing to make each remaining moment count? And as we wait, what are we doing to produce a long-term kingdom impact?

[Discover more about Jesus coming soon in Hebrews 10:36–37, Revelation 2:16, and Revelation 3:11. Read about the kingdom of God (heaven) being near in Matthew 3:2, Mark 1:15, and Luke 21:31.]

Today's reading comes from *A New Heaven and a New Earth: 40 Practical Insights from John's Book of Revelation.*

THE 40-DAY BIBLE STUDY SERIES

Which book do you want to read next in the 40-Day Bible Study Series?

- Dear Theophilus (the Gospel of **Luke**, formerly That You May Know)
- Dear Theophilus, **Acts** (formerly Tongues of Fire)
- Dear Theophilus, **Isaiah** (formerly For Unto Us)
- Dear Theophilus, **Minor Prophets** (formerly Return to Me)
- Dear Theophilus, **Job** (formerly I Hope in Him)
- Living Water (**John**)
- Love Is Patient (**1 and 2 Corinthians**)

The 40-Day Bible Study Series

- A New Heaven and a New Earth (**Revelation**)
- Love One Another (**1, 2, and 3 John**)
- Run with Perseverance (**Hebrews**)

For a list of all Peter's books, go to PeterDeHaan.com/books.

FOR SMALL GROUPS, SUNDAY SCHOOL, AND CLASSES

Living a Faith that Matters makes an ideal six-week Bible study discussion guide for small groups, Sunday School, and classes. To prepare for the conversation, read one chapter of this book each weekday, Monday through Friday.

- Week 1: read Days 1 through 5.
- Week 2: read Days 6 through 10.
- Week 3: read Days 11 through 15.
- Week 4: read Days 16 through 20.
- Week 5: read Days 21 through 25.
- Week 6: read Days 26 through 30.

When you get together, discuss the questions at the end of each chapter. The leader can use all the

For Small Groups, Sunday School, and Classes

questions to guide this discussion or pick which ones to focus on.

Before beginning the discussion, pray as a group. Ask for Holy Spirit insight and clarity.

As you discuss each chapter's questions:

- Look for how this can grow your understanding of the Bible.
- Evaluate how this can expand your faith.
- Consider what you need to change in how you live your life.

End by asking God to help you apply what you've learned.

May God bless you as you read and study his word.

IF YOU'RE NEW TO THE BIBLE

Each entry in this book contains Bible references. These can guide you if you want to learn more. If you're not familiar with the Bible, here's an overview to get you started, give some context, and minimize confusion.

First, the Bible is a collection of works written by various authors over several centuries. Think of the Bible as a diverse anthology of godly communication. It contains historical accounts, poetry, songs, letters of instruction and encouragement, messages from God sent through his representatives, and prophecies.

Most versions of the Bible have sixty-six books grouped into two sections: The Old Testament and the New Testament. The Old Testament contains

If You're New to the Bible

thirty-nine books that precede and anticipate Jesus. The New Testament includes twenty-seven books and covers Jesus's life and the work of his followers.

The reference notations in the Bible, such as Romans 3:23, are analogous to line numbers in a Shakespearean play. They serve as a study aid. Since the Bible is much longer and more complex than a play, its reference notations are more involved.

As already mentioned, the Bible is an amalgam of books, or sections, such as Genesis, Psalms, John, Acts, or 1 Peter. These are the names given to them, over time, based on the piece's author, audience, or purpose.

In the 1200s, each book was divided into chapters, such as Acts 2 or Psalm 23. In the 1500s, the chapters were further subdivided into verses, such as John 3:16. Let's use this as an example.

The name of the book (John) appears first, followed by the chapter number (3), a colon, and then the verse number (16). Sometimes called a chapter-verse reference notation, this helps people quickly find a specific text regardless of their version of the Bible.

Although the goal was to place these chapter and verse divisions at logical breaks, they sometimes

If You're New to the Bible

seem arbitrary. Therefore, it's a good practice to read what precedes and follows each passage you're studying since the text before or after it may contain relevant insight into the portion you're exploring.

Here's how to look up a specific passage in the Bible based on its reference: Most Bibles contain a table of contents, which gives the page number for the beginning of each book. Start there. Locate the book you want to read, and turn to that page. Then flip forward to the chapter you want. Last, skim that chapter to locate the specific verse.

If you want to read online, enter the reference into BibleGateway.com or BibleHub.com. Also check out the YouVersion app.

Learn more about the greatest book ever written at ABibleADay.com, which provides a Bible blog, summaries of the books of the Bible, a dictionary of Bible terms, Bible reading plans, and other resources.

ABOUT PETER DEHAAN

Peter DeHaan, PhD, wants to change the world one word at a time. His books and blog posts discuss God, the Bible, and church, geared toward spiritual seekers and church dropouts. Many people feel church has let them down, and Peter seeks to encourage them as they search for a place to belong.

But he's not afraid to ask tough questions or make religious people squirm. He's not trying to be provocative. Instead, he seeks truth, even if it makes people uncomfortable. Peter urges Christians to push past the status quo and reexamine how they practice their faith in every part of their lives.

Peter earned his doctorate, awarded with high distinction, from Trinity College of the Bible and Theological Seminary. He lives with his wife in beautiful Southwest Michigan and wrangles crossword puzzles in his spare time.

A lifelong student of Scripture, Peter wrote the 1,000-page website ABibleADay.com to encourage people to explore the Bible, the greatest book ever written. His popular blog, at PeterDeHaan.com, addresses biblical Christianity to build a faith that matters.

Read his blog, receive his newsletter, and learn more at
 PeterDeHaan.com.

BOOKS BY PETER DEHAAN

40-Day Bible Study Series

Dear Theophilus (Luke, formerly That You May Know)

Dear Theophilus, Acts (formerly Tongues of Fire)

Dear Theophilus, Isaiah (formerly For Unto Us)

Dear Theophilus, Minor Prophets (formerly Return to Me)

Dear Theophilus, Job (formerly I Hope in Him)

Living Water (John)

Love Is Patient (1 and 2 Corinthians)

A New Heaven and a New Earth (Revelation)

Love One Another (1, 2, and 3 John)

Run with Perseverance (Hebrews)

Holiday Celebration Devotional Series

The Advent of Jesus (Advent devotional)

The Passion of Jesus (Lenten devotional)

The Victory of Jesus (Easter devotional)

The Ministry of Jesus (Ordinary Time devotional)

Bible Character Sketches Series

Women of the Bible

The Friends and Foes of Jesus

Old Testament Sinners and Saints

More Old Testament Sinners and Saints

Heroes and Heavies of the Apocrypha

Visiting Churches Series

52 Churches

The 52 Churches Workbook

More Than 52 Churches

The More Than 52 Churches Workbook

Visiting Online Church

Shopping for Church

Other Books

Jesus's Broken Church

Martin Luther's 95 Theses

The Christian Church's LGBTQ Failure

Bridging the Sacred-Secular Divide

Beyond Psalm 150

How Big Is Your Tent?

For the latest list of all Peter's books, go to PeterDeHaan.com/books.

Printed in Great Britain
by Amazon